Romantic

Real Repertoire

Selected and edited by Christine Brown

Contents

Grade

Faber Music Bloomsbury House 74–77 Great Russell Street London WC1B 3DA

in association with

Trinity College London 89 Albert Embankment London SE1 7TP

THE ROMANTIC PERIOD

The composers of the Romantic period inherited the Classical forms and added an element of self expression, often taking their inspiration from art, literature or the wilder aspects of nature.

THE PIANO

The piano in the Romantic period provided an ideal vehicle for composers to express their personal feelings. The instrument now had a range of five and a half octaves, two pedals and, after the introduction of the metal rather than the wooden frame, a much wider dynamic range.

THE COMPOSERS AND THEIR PIECES

JOHANNES BRAHMS (1833–1897) was born and spent his childhood in Hamburg. Later he travelled widely meeting Joachim, Liszt and the Schumanns. He wrote many large-scale works for orchestra, much choral and chamber music and a substantial amount of piano music including two concertos requiring great virtuosity from the soloist. On one of his visits to Vienna, where he eventually settled, he wrote a set of sixteen waltzes for piano duet and published them with two arrangements by himself for piano solo. This edition of the *Waltz in B minor* is the simpler version for smaller hands.

FRYDERYK CHOPIN (1810–1849), sometimes called "the poet of the piano", was born in Poland of mixed French and Polish parentage and began to compose at the age of six. After leaving school he attended the Warsaw Conservatory studying piano and composition. He made his debut as a pianist in Vienna and on the publication of his *Variations on Là ci darem la mano* Op. 2 (1827), which he had played in his recital programme, Schumann wrote, "Hats off, gentlemen, a genius!" Almost all Chopin's works are for the piano and include waltzes, a set of 24 preludes (one in each major and minor key), sonatas, concertos and, in a Polish style, polonaises and mazurkas.

GABRIEL FAURÉ (1845–1924) was born in Pamiers and trained as a church musician at the École Niedermeyer in Paris. The three *Romances sans paroles* Op.17 (1863) were written while Fauré was still a student, but even so his own individual style is recognisable. He had a gift for writing beautiful melodies and he developed a very individual harmonic idiom with subtle changes of tonality. His piano pieces and songs have earned a permanent place in the repertoire along with his chamber music and the *Requiem* for choir and orchestra.

JOHN FIELD (1782–1837) was born in Dublin and became famous as a pianist and a composer. His father brought the ten-year-old prodigy to London where he was apprenticed to Clementi, the renowned pianist, publisher and piano manufacturer. Clementi taught the boy both piano and composition and also used him to demonstrate the new instruments. Field is remembered today as the inventor of the *Nocturne* of which he published nineteen. These pieces exploit the ability of the new pianos to allow melodies (often decorated by chromatically inflected figurations) to sing above widely spaced left hand harmonies, which are supported by the sustaining pedal.

EDVARD GRIEG (1843–1907), Norway's most famous composer, was first taught the piano by his mother, who was an excellent pianist. He was then sent to Leipzig to study at the Conservatory with Moscheles and Reinecke. His career began in Bergen, then he moved to Copenhagen where he met the singer Nina Hagerup whom he married. Most of his compositions were songs or piano music, including the famous *Piano Concerto* Op.16 (1868) which Liszt read at sight when Grieg visited him in Italy. The *Poetic Tone-Pictures* were early works, published when Grieg was only 21, while the ten sets of *Lyric Pieces* were written over a long period and show his great skill in writing for the instrument.

ALEXANDER ILYNSKY (1859–1920), born in Russia, studied the piano with Kullak and composition with Bargiel in Berlin. He returned home to graduate from the St. Petersburg Conservatory and then undertook a number of teaching appointments. He is remembered for the opera *The Fountain of Bakhchisary* (based on a work by Pushkin), several music textbooks and some instrumental pieces such as the beautiful *Berceuse* for piano.

FELIX MENDELSSOHN (1809–1847) was born into a rich and famous family and received an excellent education from distinguished private tutors in Berlin. He showed exceptional talent at music, art and literature. An accomplished pianist himself, his eight books of *Songs without Words* show a marvellous understanding of the instrument, exploiting its ability to make melodies sing and to sustain harmonies. On a larger scale he wrote two piano concertos, symphonies, overtures and oratorios.

ROBERT SCHUMANN (1810–1856), the son of a bookseller, was born in Saxony and began to compose while still at school. While studying law in Leipzig he had piano lessons from the famous teacher Friedrich Wieck and decided on a career in music, not as a pianist because he had injured a hand, but as a composer and critic. After a long wait and legal proceedings to get the necessary permission, he married Clara Wieck, the pianist daughter of his former teacher. Clara proved to be the inspiration for many of his piano works including the *Piano Concerto* Op.54 which she performed all over Europe. He expressed himself most perfectly in the small pieces which were grouped together in sets such as *Scenes of Childhood* Op.15 (1838) and *Woodland Scenes* Op.82 (1848-9).

PYOTR ILYICH TCHAIKOVSKY (1840–1893) is often described as the most popular composer of classical music. His own compositions owe much to the haunting beauty of the Russian folk music which he heard as a small child. When he was eight the family moved to St Petersburg where he attended the School of Jurisprudence. After a period in the civil service he enrolled in the newly opened Conservatory in that city and then moved to Moscow to teach harmony at the Conservatory there. He is chiefly remembered for his six symphonies, piano and violin concertos, operas and music for ballets. His *Album for the Young* Op.39 (1878) is a set of relatively easy piano pieces which he wrote while relaxing after completing his fourth symphony and his opera *Eugene Onegin*.

WALTZ IN B MINOR

Op.39 No.11

Johannes Brahms
(1833–1897)

* Play all acciaccaturas and grace notes before the beat.
The suggested pedalling is editorial.

MAZURKA IN G MINOR

Op.67 No.2

Fryderyk Chopin
(1810–1849)

PRELUDE IN B MINOR

Op.28 No.6

Fryderyk Chopin
(1810–1849)

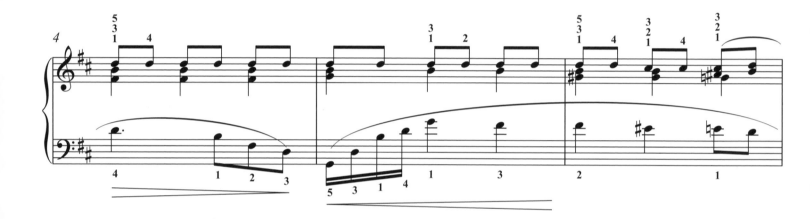

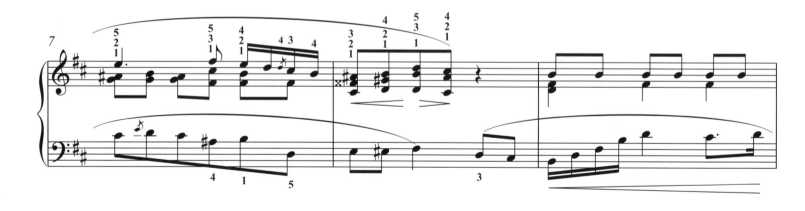

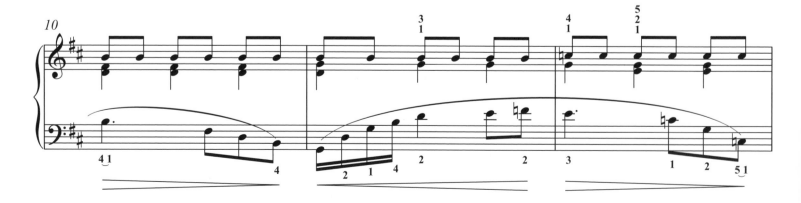

The pedal marks are from the original edition.

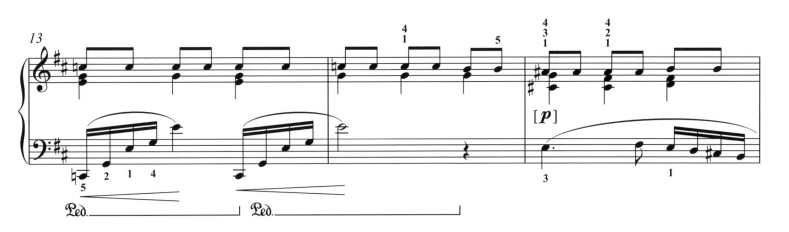

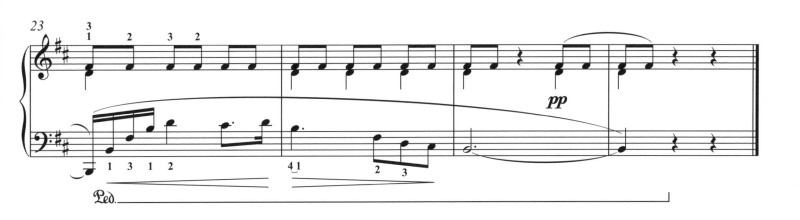

WALTZ IN C SHARP MINOR

Op.64 No.2

Fryderyk Chopin
(1810–1849)

The pedal marks are based on those of Chopin in the original edition and in the manuscript.

* Play the grace notes on the beat.

Tempo I

NOCTURNE IN B FLAT

John Field
(1782–1837)

* Play the grace note as a semiquaver on the beat.
The suggested pedalling is editorial.

BERCEUSE

Op.13 No.7

Alexander Ilynsky
(1859–1920)

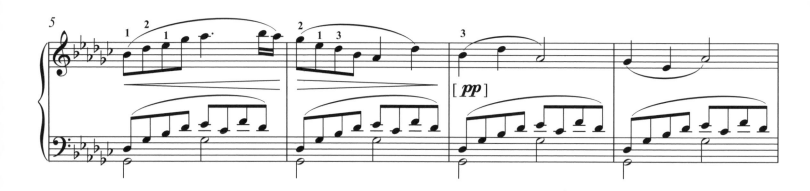

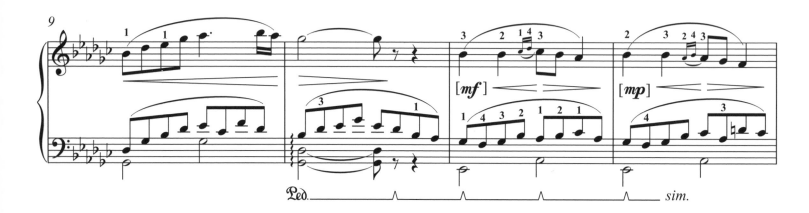

The pedalling is editorial. Play grace notes before the beat and the acciaccatura on the beat.

BUTTERFLY

from Lyric Pieces, Op.43 No.1

Edvard Grieg
(1843–1907)

24

POETIC TONE PICTURE

Op.3 No.1

Edvard Grieg
(1843–1907)

* Omit the lower R.H. E if necessary.

PUCK

from Lyric Pieces, Op.71 No.3

Edvard Grieg
(1843–1907)

ROMANCE SANS PAROLES

Op.17 No.3

Gabriel Fauré
(1845–1924)

The pedalling is editorial.

MUSICAL SKETCH

No.2

Felix Mendelssohn
(1809–1847)

The pedal marks are original.

VENETIAN GONDOLA SONG

from Songs without Words, Op.19 No.6

Felix Mendelssohn
(1809–1847)

More pedalling can be added as suggested in the opening bars.

FANTASY DANCE

from Album-leaves, Op.124 No.5

Robert Schumann
(1810–1856)

PERFECT HAPPINESS

from Scenes of Childhood, Op.15 No.5

Robert Schumann
(1810–1856)

The three pedal marks are Schumann's but more could be used as suggested in the first two bars.

SOLITARY FLOWERS

from Woodland Scenes, Op.82 No.3

Robert Schumann
(1810–1856)

The pedal marks are original.

SONG OF THE LARK

from Album for the Young, Op.39 No.22

Pyotr Ilyich Tchaikovsky
(1840–1893)

EDITOR'S NOTE

The pieces in *Romantic Real Repertoire* have been selected to provide intermediate pianists with enjoyable music for private study or for performance in concerts, festivals and examinations. There is a wide choice as the pieces vary in technical difficulty, length, tempo, key, character and mood.

The fingering and pedalling marks provided by the composers have been retained, with additions where necessary for consistency. The metronome marks in brackets are editorial and have been given as a guide but are not obligatory. Any other editorial suggestions are shown either in brackets or, in a few places to aid clarity, by dotted lines.

I hope that the study of these fine pieces will bring much pleasure to pianists and that they will then be encouraged to explore other works by the composers of the Romantic Era.

Christine Brown

© 2005 by Faber Music Ltd and Trinity College London
First published in 2005 by Faber Music Ltd
in association with Trinity College London
Bloomsbury House 74–77 Great Russell Street London WC1B 3DA
Cover design by Sue Clarke
Original handwriting by Kathy Baxendale
Music processed by Jackie Leigh
Printed in England by Caligraving Ltd

ISBN10: 0-571-52335-8
EAN13: 978-0-571-52335-1

To buy Faber Music or Trinity publications or to find out about the full range of titles available please contact your local music retailer or Faber Music sales enquiries:

Faber Music Ltd, Burnt Mill, Elizabeth Way, Harlow CM20 2HX
Tel: +44 (0)1279 82 89 82   Fax: +44 (0)1279 82 89 83
sales@fabermusic.com   fabermusic.com   trinitycollege.co.uk